Hymns

for

Little Children.

To my dear neices
from their Aunt
Georgina Meyler
August 1853 -

Hymns for Little Children.

Hymns for Little Children.

by

✠

Cecil Frances Alexander

BY THE AUTHOR OF

'THE LORD OF THE FOREST," "VERSES FOR HOLY SEASONS,"
AND "THE BARON'S LITTLE DAUGHTER."

"OUT OF THE MOUTH OF BABES AND SUCKLINGS THOU HAST
PERFECTED PRAISE,"—S. MATT. xxi. 16.

Fifth Edition.

LONDON:

JOSEPH MASTERS, ALDERSGATE STREET,
AND NEW BOND STREET.

MDCCCLII.

11427.9

1853, April 13.

LONDON:
PRINTED BY JOSEPH MASTERS AND CO.,
ALDERSGATE STREET.

TO

MY LITTLE GODSONS,

I INSCRIBE THESE SIMPLE LINES,

HOPING THAT

HE LANGUAGE OF VERSE, WHICH CHILDREN LOVE,

MAY HELP TO IMPRESS ON THEIR MINDS

WHAT THEY ARE,

WHAT I HAVE PROMISED FOR THEM,

AND

WHAT THEY MUST SEEK TO BE.

C. F. H.

Notice.

THE title of this little book shows it to be of a kind which stands in as small need as any of preface or explanation. Children, and those interested in children, will feel at once whether it suits them or not. These few lines, however, are prefixed, because the writer of the Hymns wished for some kind of clerical *imprimatur*, and the Clergyman to whom she applied, thinks and hopes that they will not only be found useful in the way which she earnestly desires, but will also win a high place for themselves in the estimation of all who know how to value true poetry and primitive devotion.

It seems right to add, that the profits of the publication, if any, will be applied to the support of a school for deaf and dumb children maintained altogether by voluntary offerings, in a small town in the north of Ireland.

J. K.

HURSLEY, MARCH 28, 1848.

Contents.

	PAGE
MORNING HYMN	13
EVENING HYMN	16
HYMN OF THE HOLY TRINITY	18
HOLY BAPTISM	19

THE FIRST PROMISE—

To renounce the devil and all his works	21
The pomps and vanity of this wicked world	22
And all the sinful lusts of the flesh	24

THE SECOND PROMISE—

To believe all the Articles of the Christian Faith.

OF THE CREED—

I believe in GOD the FATHER Almighty	26
Maker of heaven and earth	27
And in JESUS CHRIST His only SON, our LORD	28
Who was conceived by the HOLY GHOST, Born of the Virgin Mary	30

PAGE

Suffered under Pontius Pilate, Was crucified, dead
and buried 31
He descended into hell; The third day He rose again
from the dead 33
He ascended into heaven, And sitteth at the right
hand of GOD the FATHER Almighty; From thence
He shall come to judge the quick and the dead . 34
I believe in the HOLY GHOST 35
The Holy Catholic Church 37
The Communion of Saints 39
The Forgiveness of sins 41
The Resurrection of the body 42
And the life everlasting 43

THE THIRD PROMISE—

To keep GOD's holy will and commandments, and
walk in the same all the days of my life.

OF THE COMMANDMENTS—

I. 45
II. 46
III. 48
IV. 49
V. 50
VI. 52
VII. 53
VIII. 54
IX. 55
X. 57

PRAYER—

My good Child, know this, that thou art not able to
do these things of thyself, nor to walk in the com-
mandments of GOD, and to serve Him, without His
special grace; which thou must learn at all times to
call for by diligent Prayer 59

PAGE

THE LORD'S PRAYER—

Our FATHER, Which art in heaven 60

Hallowed be Thy Name 61

Thy kingdom come 63

Thy will be done in earth, As it is in heaven . . 64

Give us this day our daily bread 65

And forgive us our trespasses, As we forgive them
that trespass against us 67

And lead us not into temptation 68

But deliver us from evil 70

Therefore I say, Amen, so be it 71

Hymns For Little Children.

1.

Morning Hymn.

Now the dreary night is done,
Comes again the glorious sun,
Crimson clouds, and silver white,
Wait upon his breaking light.

Glistening in the garden beds,
Flowers lift up their dewy heads,
And the shrill cock claps his wings,
And the merry lark upsprings:

B

14   HYMNS FOR CHILDREN.

When the eastern sky is red,
I, too, lift my little head.
When the lark sings loud and gay,
I, too, rise to praise and pray.

SAVIOUR, to Thy cottage home
Once the daylight used to come;
Thou hast ofttimes seen it break
Brightly o'er that eastern lake.

Child of Mary, Thou dost know,
What of danger, joy, or woe,
Shall to-day my portion be,
Let me meet it all in Thee.

Thou wast meek and undefiled,
Make me holy too, and mild;
Thou didst foil the tempter's power,
Help me in temptation's hour.

Thou didst love Thy mother here,
Make me gentle, kind and dear;
Thou wast subject to her word,
Teach me to obey, O LORD.

Fretful feelings, passion, pride,
Never did with Thee abide;
Make me watch myself to-day,
That they lead me not astray.

With Thee, LORD, I would arise,
To Thee look with opening eyes,
All the day be at Thy side,
SAVIOUR, PATTERN, KING, and GUIDE.

2.

Evening Hymn.

ON the dark hill's western side
The last purple gleam has died,
Twilight to one solemn hue
Changes all, both green and blue.

In the fold and in the nest,
Birds and lambs are gone to rest;
Labour's weary task is o'er,
Closely shut the cottage door.

SAVIOUR, ere in sweet repose
I my weary eyelids close,
While my mother through the gloom
Singeth from the outer room;

While across the curtain white,
With a dim uncertain light,
On the floor the faint stars shine,
Let my latest thought be Thine.

'Twas a starry night of old,
When rejoicing Angels told
The poor shepherds of Thy birth,
GOD become a Child on earth.

Soft and quiet is the bed,
Where I lay my little head;
Thou hadst but a manger bare,
Rugged straw for pillow fair.

SAVIOUR, 'twas to win me grace,
Thou didst stoop to that poor place,
Loving with a perfect love
Child, and man, and GOD above.

Hear me as alone I lie,
Plead for me with GOD on high;
All that stained my soul to-day,
Wash it in Thy blood away.

If my slumbers broken be,
Waking let me think of Thee:
Darkness cannot make me fear,
If I feel that Thou art near.

Happy now I turn to sleep;
Thou wilt watch around me keep;
Him no danger e'er can harm,
Who lies cradled on Thine Arm.

3.

Hymn of the Holy Trinity.

WE are little Christian children,
    We can run, and talk, and play;
The Great GOD of earth and Heaven,
    Made, and keeps us every day.

We are little Christian children;
    CHRIST, the SON of GOD Most High,
With His precious blood redeemed us,
    Dying that we might not die.

We are little Christian children,
    GOD the HOLY GHOST is here,
Dwelling in our hearts, to make us
    Kind, and holy, good, and dear.

We are little Christian children,
    Saved by Him Who loved us most,
We believe in GOD Almighty,
    FATHER, SON, and HOLY GHOST.

4.

Holy Baptism.

WE were only little babies,
  Knowing neither good nor harm,
When the Priest of GOD Most Holy
  Took us gently in his arm.

And he sprinkled our young faces
  With the water clear and bright,
And he signed our SAVIOUR's token
  On our little foreheads white.

In the Name of GOD the FATHER,
  Of the SON, and HOLY GHOST,
He baptizèd us then, and made us
  Soldiers in our Master's host.

Then we promised by our sureties,
   Vowing for us solemnly,
Manfully to fight His battles,
   Gentle, kind, and good to be.

At our posts beneath His banner,
   We must watch, and strive, and pray,
By the Grace of GOD within us
   Growing better every day.

For the little flowers grow brightly
   In the early morning dew,
And when GOD's good SPIRIT feeds them,
   Children's hearts grow holy too.

We must keep our early promise,
   We must guard what He has given,
Till the LORD, Who loved and saved us,
   Take us to our home in Heaven.

5.

The First Promise.

Do no sinful action,
  Speak no angry word,
Ye belong to JESUS,
  Children of the LORD.

CHRIST is kind and gentle,
  CHRIST is pure and true,
And His little children
  Must be holy too.

There's a wicked spirit
  Watching round you still,
And he tries to tempt you
  To all harm and ill.

But ye must not hear him
  Though 'tis hard for you
To resist the evil,
  And the good to do.

For ye promised truly
  In your infant days,
To renounce him wholly,
  And forsake his ways.

Ye are new-born Christians,
  Ye must learn to fight
With the bad within you,
  And to do the right.

CHRIST is your own Master,
  He is good and true,
And His little children
  Must be holy too.

6.

THE POMPS AND VANITY OF THIS WICKED WORLD.

AT Nazareth in olden time,
  A peasant's cottage stood,
Where Joseph the poor carpenter
  Toiled for his daily food.

An humble Virgin lived with him,
   Beneath that lowly shed,
And there, her Son, our SAVIOUR CHRIST,
   In poverty was bred.

He had no glory here on earth,
   No riches and no state;
His Christian children must not care
   For being rich or great.

Fine clothes, fine houses, pretty things,
   That please our longing eyes,
Would only make our hearts forget
   Our treasure in the skies.

It would be wrong on pomp or dress
   To spend our thoughts or hours;
Another lesson CHRIST hath taught,
   Showing the simple flowers.

There's not a yellow buttercup
   Returning with the spring
But it can boast a golden crown,
   As bright as any king.

The red rose and the lily fair,
   That charm our summer's day;
There's not a lady in the land
   As finely dressed as they.

They feel no proud, no foolish thoughts,
    Because they are so fair;
They wish for nothing, quite content
    With sunshine and sweet air.

GOD gave to them their colours bright,
    To us, faith, hope, and love,
And bade us fear the things of earth,
    And seek the things above.

7.

AND ALL THE SINFUL LUSTS OF THE FLESH.

WE were washed in holy water,
    We were set CHRIST's Church within,
Gifted with His HOLY SPIRIT,
    And forgiven all our sin.

But though born again, and granted
    Grace to pray and strength to fight,
Still remains our sinful nature,
    Weakened, not extinguished quite.

Sinful thoughts of pride and passion,
    Greedy wishes, selfish care,
In our human hearts lie hidden,
    Ready to awaken there.

Still the wrong way will seem pleasant,
  Still the right way will seem hard;
All our life we shall be tempted,
  We must ever be on guard.

We are soldiers doing battle,
  Day by day, and hour by hour,
Each one with his own temptations
  Striving in the SPIRIT's power;

Still that SPIRIT stronger groweth
  In the hearts that hold It fast;
He will help us, teach us, crown us,
  More than conqu'rors at the last.

8.

The Second Promise.

TO BELIEVE ALL THE ARTICLES OF THE CHRISTIAN FAITH.

Of the Creed.

I BELIEVE IN GOD THE FATHER ALMIGHTY.

How good is the Almighty GOD,
   How merciful and mild,
Who is to me a FATHER dear,
   And I His favoured child.

There's no one in the whole wide earth,
   Not my own mother even,
Who loves me half as well as He,
   My FATHER high in Heaven.

Did He not give His Own dear SON,
   To die for sinful men?
To turn them from their wicked ways,
   And bring them back again;

Back to the place that they had lost,
   Back to their FATHER'S love,
Their FATHER the Great GOD of all,
·   Their home, His Heaven above!

And I am called by CHRIST'S dear Name,
   I took the solemn vow
That made me His for evermore,
   GOD is my FATHER now.

9.

MAKER OF HEAVEN AND EARTH.

ALL things bright and beautiful,
   All creatures great and small,
All things wise and wonderful,
   The LORD GOD made them all.

Each little flower that opens,
   Each little bird that sings,
He made their glowing colours,
   He made their tiny wings.

The rich man in his castle,
   The poor man at his gate,
GOD made them, high or lowly,
   And ordered their estate.

The purple-headed mountain,
  The river running by,
The sunset, and the morning,
  That brightens up the sky,

The cold wind in the winter,
  The pleasant summer sun,
The ripe fruits in the garden,
  He made them every one.

The tall trees in the greenwood,
  The meadows where we play,
The rushes by the water,
  We gather every day;—

He gave us eyes to see them,
  And lips that we might tell,
How great is GOD Almighty,
  Who has made all things well.

10.

AND IN JESUS CHRIST HIS ONLY SON OUR LORD.

WHEN we speak of the LORD JESUS,
  When His awful Name is said,
We will repeat it solemnly,
  We will bow the head.

For our LOı
And He 1
He was boı
Here He

'Twas for u
Died the
We will try
We will i

In the holy
Speaking
In our quiet
In GOD's .

JESUS CHRIS
Whensoe'ᴇ
We will repᴇ
We will bᴇ

11.

ONCE in royal David's City,
　　Stood a lowly cattle shed,
Where a mother laid her Baby,
　　In a manger for His bed.
Mary was that mother mild,
JESUS CHRIST her little child.

He came down to earth from Heaven,
　　Who is GOD and LORD of all,
And His shelter was a stable,
　　And His cradle was a stall;
With the poor, and mean, and lowly,
Lived on earth our SAVIOUR Holy.

And through all His wondrous childhood,
　　He would honour and obey,
Love and watch the lowly maiden
　　In whose gentle arms He lay.
Christian children all must be
Mild, obedient, good as He.

For He is our childhood's Pattern,
  Day by day like us He grew,
He was little, weak and helpless,
  Tears and smiles like us He knew,
And He feeleth for our sadness,
And He shareth in our gladness.

And our eyes at last shall see Him,
  Through His Own redeeming love,
For that Child so dear and gentle
  Is our LORD in Heaven above;
And He leads His children on
To the place where He is gone.

Not in that poor lowly stable,
  With the oxen standing by,
We shall see Him; but in Heaven,
  Set at GOD'S right Hand on high;
When like stars His children crowned,
All in white, shall wait around.

12.

SUFFERED UNDER PONTIUS PILATE,
WAS CRUCIFIED, DEAD, AND BURIED.

THERE is a green hill far away,
  Without a city wall,
Where the dear LORD was crucified,
  Who died to save us all.

We may not know, we cannot tell
  What pains He had to bear,
But we believe it was for us,
  He hung and suffered there.

He died that we might be forgiven,
  He died to make us good,
That we might go at last to Heaven,
  Saved by His precious Blood.

There was no other good enough
  To pay the price of sin,
He only could unlock the gate
  Of Heaven, and let us in.

O, dearly, dearly has He loved,
  And we must love Him too,
And trust in His redeeming Blood,
  And try His works to do.

13.

HE DESCENDED INTO HELL, THE THIRD DAY HE ROSE AGAIN
FROM THE DEAD.

THE rich man did of Pilate crave
　The lifeless body of the LORD,
And laid it in his own new grave;
　There all night long with spear and sword,
The Roman soldiers watched the stone,
Where the world's SAVIOUR lay alone.

But with the first day's dawning bright,
　That heavy stone was rolled away,
Two glorious Angels all in white,
　Sat where the SAVIOUR's Body lay;
The watch, the seal, were all in vain,
The LORD of Life was risen again.

There are short graves in churchyard ground,
　Where little children buried lie,
Each underneath his narrow mound,
　With stiff cold hand, and close shut eye;
Bright morning sunbeams kiss the spot,
Yet day by day they open not.

But surely as our SAVIOUR rose
    On Easter morn from Joseph's cave,
Shall all those mounds at last unclose,
    And Christian people leave the grave.
He died, He slept, He rose to be
An earnest of our victory.

LORD, Who for us so cold and deep
    Down in that garden grave hast lain,
When we like Thee must fall asleep,
    Be with us in our hour of pain,
That strengthened by Thy Grace Divine,
Alive or dead we may be Thine.

14.

HE ASCENDED INTO HEAVEN, AND SITTETH AT THE RIGHT HAND
OF GOD THE FATHER ALMIGHTY, FROM THENCE HE SHALL
COME TO JUDGE THE QUICK AND THE DEAD.

UP in Heaven, up in Heaven,
    In the bright place far away,
He Whom bad men crucified,
Sitteth at His FATHER's side,
    Till the Judgment Day.

And He loves His little children,
    And He pleadeth for them there,
Asking the Great GOD of Heaven
That their sins may be forgiven,
    And He hears their prayer.

Never more a helpless Baby,
    Born in poverty and pain,
But with awful glory crowned,
With His Angels standing round,
    He shall come again.

Then the wicked souls shall tremble,
    And the good souls shall rejoice ;
Parents, children, every one,
Then shall stand before His throne,
    And shall hear His voice.

And all faithful holy Christians,
    Who their Master's work have done,
Shall appear at His right hand,
And inherit the fair land
    That His love has won.

15.

I BELIEVE IN THE HOLY GHOST.

I KNEW a little sickly child ;
    The long long summer's day,
When all the world was green and bright,
    Alone in bed he lay.
There used to come a little dove
    Before his window small,
And sing to him with her sweet voice,
    Out of the fir tree tall.

And when the sick child better grew,
　And he could crawl along,
Close to that window he would creep,
　And listen to her song;
And he was gentle in his speech,
　And quiet at his play;
He would not for the world have made
　That sweet bird fly away.

There is a Holy Dove that sings
　To every Christian child,
That whispers to his little heart
　A song as sweet and mild.
It is the HOLY SPIRIT of GOD,
　That speaks his soul within,
That leads him on to all things good,
　And holds him back from sin.

And he must hear that still small Voice,
　Nor tempt It to depart,
The SPIRIT great and wonderful,
　That whispers to his heart;
He must be pure, and good, and true,
　Must strive, and watch, and pray,
For unresisted sin at last
　Will drive that Dove away.

16.

LITTLE children must be quiet,
When to Holy Church they go,
They must sit with serious faces,
Must not play or whisper low.

For the Church is GOD's Own Temple,
Where men go for praise and prayer,
And the Great GOD will not love them
Who forget His Presence there.

They were little Jewish children,
Who within the temple cried,
" Honour to the Son of David,"
Standing at our SAVIOUR's side.

How much more should Christian children
Know His name and praise Him too,
Who of His Own Church are members,
Sons of GOD, and born anew.

They must walk in reverent order,
Stand for praise, and kneel for prayer,
For the Church is GOD's Own Temple,
And His presence dwelleth there.

D

16.*

THE faithful men of every land,
  Who CHRIST'S Own rule obey,
The holy dead of every time—
  The Church of CHRIST, are they.

The Saints who die, and leave us now,
  The Good of long ago,
Women, and men, and children young,
  Still living here below :

Who have the same eternal hope,
  The same unceasing care,
One universal hymn of praise,
  One general voice of prayer :

All members of one body vast,
  With JESUS for their Head,
And sacraments whereby their souls
  Are born again, and fed :

And Bishops good to order them,
  And Priests to train and teach,—
This is the holy Church, wherein
  We have our places each.

Since we are members, then, of CHRIST,
   How holy should we be,
How faithful to obey our Head,
   In truth and purity!

Since we are all made one in Him,
   How gentle should we prove,
How peaceful in our ways and words!
   How tender in our love.

So shall our Head, at all times near,
   Dwell in His members blest,
So lead us in His Church on earth,
   Safe to His Church at rest.

17.

THE COMMUNION OF SAINTS.

THE Saints of GOD are holy men,
   And women good, and children dear,
All those who ever loved the LORD,
   Who live in faith and fear.

They are not all together now,
   For some are dead, and gone before
And some are striving still on earth,
   Their trial is not o'er.

Great numbers are they of all states,
 And born in every place and land,
Who never saw each other's face,
 Nor touched each other's hand.

But they are all made one in CHRIST,
 They love each other tenderly,
The old and young, the rich and poor
 Of that great company.

CHRIST's little children, called His Own
 And saved by His redeeming Blood,
They must be little Saints on earth,
 And all the Saints are good.

They must not fight or disobey,
 For Saints do never things like these ;
They must be holy, meek, and mild,
 And try the LORD to please.

And there shall come a glorious Day,
 When all the good Saints every one,
Shall meet within their FATHER's home,
 And stand before His Throne.

18.

THE FORGIVENESS OF SINS.

ONCE in baptismal waters bright
He washed our sinful spirits white,
   Forgave us once for all.
But we have sometimes sinned since then;
Now who shall make us clean again?
   And who shall hear our call?

There is One only Who forgives,
CHRIST Who was born, Who died, Who lives,
   Pleading beside the Throne;
Who hath His HOLY SPIRIT sent,
To bless that precious Sacrament
   That made us first His Own.

Who when His Holy Church within,
Confession sad of all our sin
   We make on bended knee,
Accepts the penitential prayer,
And bids His Minister declare
   Our pardon full and free.

He only hears the sinner's cry,
He only dries the mourner's eye,
   No father half so mild,
Not half so kind a mother's kiss,
When pardoning what is done amiss,
   She soothes her sorrowing child.

D 2

We must take heed to cast no stain
On souls He bought with so much pain,
  And with His blood made pure;
And we must trust to Him alone,
Who did for all our guilt atone,
  Who made our pardon sure.

19.

THE RESURRECTION OF THE BODY.

WITHIN the churchyard, side by side,
  Are many long low graves,
And some have stones set over them,—
  On some the green grass waves.

Full many a little Christian child,
  Woman and man, lies there;
And we pass by them every time
  When we go in to prayer.

They cannot hear our footsteps come,
  They do not see us pass,
They cannot feel the bright warm sun
  That shines upon the grass.

They do not hear when the great bell
  Is ringing over head;
They cannot rise and come to Church
  With us, for they are dead.

But we believe a Day shall come,
  When all the dead will rise,
When they who sleep down in the grave,
  Will ope again their eyes.

For CHRIST our LORD was buried once,
  He died and rose again,
He conquered death, He left the grave,
  And so will Christian men.

So when the friends we loved the best
  Lie in their churchyard bed,
We must not cry too bitterly
  Over the happy dead;

Because for our dear SAVIOUR's sake,
  Our sins are all forgiven,
And Christians only fall asleep,
  To wake again in Heaven.

20.

AND THE LIFE EVERLASTING.

EVERY morning the red sun
  Rises warm and bright,
But the evening cometh on,
  And the dark cold night.
There's a bright land far away,
Where 'tis never ending day.

Every spring the sweet young flowers
   Open bright and gay,
Till the chilly autumn hours
   Wither them away.
There's a land we have not seen,
Where the trees are always green.

Little birds sing songs of praise
   All the summer long,
But in colder shorter days
   They forget their song.
There's a place where Angels sing
Ceaseless praises to their King.

CHRIST our LORD is ever near
   Those who follow Him,
But we cannot see Him here,
   For our eyes are dim.
There is a most happy place,
Where men always see His face.

Who shall go to that bright land?
   All who do the right:
Holy children there shall stand,
   In their robes of white,
For that Heaven so bright and blest,
Is our everlasting rest.

21.

The Third Promise.

TO KEEP GOD'S HOLY WILL AND COMMANDMENTS, AND WALK
IN THE SAME ALL THE DAYS OF MY LIFE.

Of the Commandments.

I.

THERE is One GOD, but One alone,
  He made all things in earth and Heaven;
To Him all love and praise are due,
  All worship must be given.

The little birds sing happy songs,
  The flowers grow brightly everywhere,
They do not know the Great LORD GOD,
  Who made them all so fair.

But we are not like senseless flowers,
  We are not like the little birds,
For we can love Him with our hearts,
  And praise Him with our words.

O ! if the great Almighty GOD
   Will hear the prayers that children pray,
If He will let us love His Name,
   And serve Him day by day,

If we may turn and cling to Him,
   Before Whose face the Angels fall,
Sure we must give Him our whole hearts,
   And love Him best of all.

22.

II.

THERE are strange countries far away,
   Where GOD's Name is unknown,
Where children live who say their prayers
   To gods of wood and stone.

But Christian children go to Church,
   They kneel at home in prayer,
And GOD, Who is a Spirit, hears
   And answers everywhere.

His ear is open to their call,
   In childhood, age, and youth,
And they must always worship Him
   In spirit and in truth.

They must not think of other things,
  Light toys, or merry play,
When they are listening to GOD's word,
  Or kneeling down to pray.

For they who worship at GOD's throne,
  With hearts so dull and dim,
Make idols of their foolish thoughts,
· And love them more than Him.

They may not kneel to any form,
  Or picture that man paints,
Of CHRIST, or of His Mother dear,
  Or of His blessed Saints.

They may not worship nor bow down
  To cross of stone or wood,
Though it be our redemption's sign,—
  Such worship is not good.

For we must pray to GOD alone,
  Who is in Heaven on high,
Who is on earth with us unseen,
  Who always hears our cry.

23.

III.

Hush! little Christian child,
   Speak not that Holy Name,
Not with a laughing lip,
   Not in thy playful game;
For the Great GOD of all
   Heareth each word we say,
He will remember it
   In the great Judgment Day.

Hush!—for His hosts unseen
   Are watching over thee,
His Angels spread their wings,
   Thy shelter kind to be.
Wilt thou, with words profane,
   Rash, and undutiful,
Scatter thine Angel guards,
   Glorious and beautiful?

Honour GOD's Holy Name,
   Speak It with thought and care,
Sing to It holy hymns,
   Breathe It in earnest prayer;
But not with sudden cry,
   In thy light joy or pain,
"GOD will hold guilty all
   Who take His Name in vain."

24.

IV.

PUT the spade and wheel away,
Do no weary work to-day;
Let the way-worn horse go free,
And the field uncultured be;
Leave the flail beside the corn,
All must rest on Sunday morn.
For the LORD, Who died to save,
Rose to-day from Joseph's grave,
And with rest and holy mirth,
We will keep His feast on earth.
Hark—I hear the sweet Church bells,
And their quiet music tells,
How to keep CHRIST's holiday
In the happiest fittest way:
How His children here may meet,
All in saintly service sweet,
And in presence of their LORD,
Sing His praise and hear His word,
With our fathers and our mothers,
With our sisters and our brothers,
To the holy Church we go,
The dear Church of high and low,
Where the poor man meanly dressed,
Is as welcome as the best.

E

And the rich and poor may gather,
Kneeling to their common FATHER :—
Yea, our risen LORD is there,
Listening kindly to our prayer,—
Thus should Christian people all
Hold their Master's festival ;
Thus with joyous rest and praise,
His Own children keep His days.

25.

V.

LITTLE birds sleep sweetly
   In their soft round nests,
Crouching in the cover
   Of their mothers' breasts.

Little lambs lie quiet,
   All the summer night,
With their old ewe mothers,
   Warm, and soft, and white.

But more sweet and quiet
   Lie our little heads,
With our own dear mothers
   Sitting by our beds.

And their soft sweet voices
   Sing our hush-a-bies,
While the room grows darker
· As we shut our eyes,

And we play at evening
   Round our father's knees,
Birds are not so merry,
   Singing on the trees :

Lambs are not so happy,
   Mid the meadow flowers;
They have play and pleasure,
   But not love like ours.

But the heart that's loving,
   Works of love will do;
Those we dearly cherish,
   We must honour too :

To our father's teaching
   Listen day by day,
And our mother's bidding
· Cheerfully obey.

For when in His childhood
   Our dear LORD was here,
He too was obedient
   To His Mother dear.

And His little children
Must be good as He,
Gentle, and submissive,
As He used to be.

26.

VL

Do not quarrel, do not chide;
  You must love each other:
Every comrade at your side
  Is your Christian brother:
You have all been born anew;
Love and peace are fit for you.

Ye became by that new birth
  To the LORD most holy,
And His sainted ones on earth
  Peaceful are and lowly.
Ye are Saints, and ye must be
Worthy of such company.

Give not back the hasty blow,
  Though 'tis given wrongly;
Let the foolish scoffer go,
  Though he tempt thee strongly;
Keep thy gentle LORD in mind,
Who was always meek and kind.

He gave back no angry word,
　When they did offend Him;
He that was the Angels' LORD,
　Called none to defend Him,
Not when hated and abused,
Scorned, and spitted on, and bruised.

But He suffered patiently
　Pain and cruel chiding:
Meek and patient you must be,
　In His Church abiding;
Pride and anger would be shame
For the Saints who bear His Name.

27.

VII.

I LOVE the little snowdrop flower,
　The first in all the year,
Without a stain upon its leaf,
　So snowy white and clear.

I love a little modest child,
　That speaketh quietly,
That blushes up to its blue eyes,
　And hardly answers me.

I sometimes think the Church's Saints
  Are flowers so fair and bright,
And that her little children are
  Her snowdrops sweet and white.

For pure of heart, and innocent,
  And teachable, and mild,
And modest in its ways and words,
  Should be a Christian child.

I do not like a loud rough tone,
  A look too boldly set,
A greedy hand outstretched to seize
  Whatever it can get.

I'd rather meet with downcast eyes,
  Sweet voices low and faint;
For gentleness and modesty
  Become a little Saint.

28.

VIII.

ON the goods that are not thine,
  Little Christian, lay no finger;
Round thy neighbours' better things
  Let no wistful glances linger.

Pilfer not the smallest thing,
　Touch it not, howe'er thou need it,
Though the owner have enough,
　Though he know it not, nor heed it.

Taste not the forbidden fruit,
　Though resistance be a trial;
Grasping hand and roving eye,
　Early teach them self-denial.

Upright heart and honest name
　To the poorest are a treasure,
Better than illgotten wealth,
　Better far than pomp and pleasure.

Poor and needy though thou art,
　Gladly take what GOD has given,
With clean hand and humble heart,
　Passing through the world to Heaven.

29.

IX.

O CHRISTIAN child! in CHRIST'S Own Church
　So late baptized and born anew,
Let all thy thoughts be upright thoughts,
　Let all thy words be true.

The little lips that every day
 Say prayers to GOD at morn and eve,
They were not made for wicked words,
 That injure or deceive.

The hearts where GOD'S great Spirit dwells,
 To cleanse, and teach, and sanctify,
Should never think a wicked thought,
 Should never frame a lie.

The LORD GOD sits in Heaven above,
 The GOD Who is all pure and true,
And CHRIST our LORD is at His side,
 Beholding all we do.

The wicked father of all lies,
 Goes to and fro, and watches nigh,
And he rejoices when he gets
 A Christian child to lie.

You cannot see the Holy GOD,
 Nor that bad spirit tempting you;
But you can watch, and never speak
 A word that is not true.

For CHRIST Who looks into our hearts,
 Sees all we think, hears all we say,
Will surely help us to be good,
 If we but watch and pray.

30.

X.

Saw ye never in the meadows,
  Where your little feet did pass,
Down below, the sweet white daisies
  Growing in the long green grass?

They are like to little children,
  Children bred in lowly cot,
Who are modest, meek, and quiet,
  And contented with their lot.

Saw you never lilac blossoms,
  Or acacia white and red,
Waving brightly in the sunshine,
  On the tall trees overhead?

They are like to other children,
  Children of the high and great,
Who are gracious, good, and gentle,
  Serving God in their estate.

Christian children, high and lowly,
  Try like little flowers to be.—
Day by day the tall tree-blossom
  Gives to God its fragrance free.

Day by day the little daisy
  Looks up with its yellow eye,
Never murmurs, never wishes
  It were hanging up on high.

GOD has given each his station;
  Some have riches and high place,
Some have lowly homes and labour,—
  All may have His precious Grace.

You must be content and quiet,
  Your appointed stations in;
For to envy, or to covet
  Others' goods, is mortal sin.

And the air is just as pleasant,
  And as bright the sunny sky,
To the daisy by the footpath,
  As to flowers that bloom on high.

And GOD loveth all His children,
  Rich and poor, and high, and low,
And they all shall meet in Heaven,
  Who have served Him here below.

31.

Prayer.

MY GOOD CHILD, KNOW THIS, THAT THOU ART NOT ABLE TO DO THESE
THINGS OF THYSELF, NOR TO WALK IN THE COMMANDMENTS OF
GOD AND TO SERVE HIM, WITHOUT HIS SPECIAL GRACE;
WHICH THOU MUST LEARN AT ALL TIMES TO CALL
FOR BY DILIGENT PRAYER.

WAKE, little child, the morn is gay,
　　The air is fresh and cool;
But pause awhile, and kneel to pray,
Before you go to merry play,
　　Before you go to school.

Kneel down and speak the holy words;
　　GOD loves your simple prayer,
Above the sweet songs of the birds,
The bleating of the gentle herds,
　　The flowers that scent the air.

And when the quiet evenings come,
　　And dewdrops wet the sod,
When bats and owls begin to roam,
And flocks and herds are driven home,
　　Then kneel again to GOD.

Because you need Him day and night,
　　To shield you with His arm,
To help you always to do right,
To feed your soul and give it light,
　　And keep you safe from harm.

32.

The Lord's Prayer.

OUR FATHER WHICH ART IN HEAVEN.

Is there a little orphan child,
  Father and mother gone,
Who deems himself quite desolate,
  Left in the world alone?

It is not so—while CHRIST'S Own words
  On every lip are laid,
While each a FATHER hath in Heaven,
  To cheer him and to aid.

O! let him seek the churchyard ground,
  Some quiet summer even,
When calmly on his father's grave
  Looks down the sunset heaven.

And let him gaze on the blue sky,
  And dry the tears that gather
In his dim eyes, and breathe a prayer
  Unto his other FATHER.

Ye happier children, who below
　Still share a father's love,
Remember, earthly love is taught,
　To lead to things above.

Remember, when ye court his smile,
　Or prattling climb his knee,
Ye have a FATHER ever near,
　More kind, more good than he.

Give Him a love as fond and free,
　As fully trust His might,
Hold converse with Him day by day,
　And with as great delight.

For household duties, loves, and joys,
　Losses and cares are given,
To train the sons of GOD to reach
　Their FATHER's House in Heaven.

33.

HALLOWED BE THY NAME.

HALLOWED be our FATHER's Name,
　In the hall and in the cot;
Holy hearts, delight to honour,
　Lips profane, repeat it not.

F

Hallowed be our SAVIOUR's Name,
  Of the high and of the low;
Every mouth declare His praises,
  Every knee before Him bow.

Hallowed be the SPIRIT's Name,
  Fount eternal, gentle Dove;
Him all Christians inly cherish,
  Hear His voice, and learn His love.

Hallow we our FATHER's Name,
  We, His new-born little ones,
Love It like obedient daughters,
  Honour It like duteous sons.

Hallow we our SAVIOUR's Name,
  Let our feet His temple tread,
Speak It there with praise and blessing,
  Bowing with uncovered head.

Hallow we the HOLY GHOST,
  Let Him rule our hearts within,
Seek Him, hold Him, love Him better,
  Every hour we strive with sin.

Ever hallowed be Thy Name,
  Thereby called, and therein blessed,
MAKER, SAVIOUR, kind RENEWER,
  In Thee only we have rest.

34.

THY KINGDOM COME.

WHY do we say, " Thy kingdom come ?"
  Because our KING is far away,
And till He come to us again,
  We wait, and watch, and pray.

Because some hearts are cold and hard,
  And some are traitors to His cause,
They do not honour the great KING,
  They will not keep His laws.

And we would see through all the earth
  His holy Name beloved alone,
And every knee in homage bowed
  Before His kingly Throne.

The happy dead who rest with Him
  Are ever praying the same prayer,
For when CHRIST'S kingdom comes again,
  His Saints will all be there.

But if we say these solemn words,
  And hope to share His triumph hour,
Our hearts must be His kingdom now,
  Where He alone hath power.

They must be holy, pure, and true,
Obeying CHRIST in *every* thing,
For they who own His gentle rule,
Can have no other king.

So shall our souls be ready found,
When from the country far away,
Our KING returns in glory crowned,
To hail His Sovereign sway.

35.

THY WILL BE DONE IN EARTH, AS IT IS IN HEAVEN.

THE Angels stand around Thy Throne,
And wait Thy bidding every one,
As stars around the full bright moon,
Or clouds beneath the setting sun.

Fair creatures, beautiful and bright,
They do the will of GOD on high,
His ministers to us on earth,
Unseen their white wings gliding by.

And children, too, may do GOD's will,
Each in his lowly earthly place;
For CHRIST hath said, " our Angels bright
Always behold the FATHER's Face."

LORD, when we say, " Thy will be done,"
  May heart to lip be ever true:
O! give us grace to serve Thee here,
  As gladly as the Angels do.

Like Him, the lowly Child, Who dwelt
  Where gleams the Galilean sea,
Whose meat it was to do Thy will,—
  Our Guide, our Trust, our Pattern, He.

And if Thou send us pain or grief,
  If loss or anguish e'er befall,
Still teach us, though with quivering lip,
  To say, " Thy will be done in all."

Thus did our LORD in anguish pray,
  Saying, " Not My will, LORD, but Thine:"
So kneel we at our FATHER's Feet,
  And all our wills to Him resign.

36.

GIVE US THIS DAY OUR DAILY BREAD.

THE raven builds her nest on high,
  The loud winds rock her craving brood,
The forest echoes to their cry;
  Who gives the ravens food?

The lion goeth forth to roam
   Wild sandy hills and plains among,
He leaves his little whelps at home:
   Who feeds the lion's young ?

GOD hears the hungry lions howl,
   He feeds the raven hoarse and grey:
Cares He alone for beast and fowl?
   Are we less dear than they ?

Nay, Christian Child, kneel down and own
   The Hand that feeds thee day by day,
Nor careless with thy lip alone,
   For " all things needful" pray.

GOD made thy cottage home so dear,
   Gave store enough for frugal fare;
If richer homes have better cheer,
   'Twas GOD Who sent it there.

But better far than garners stored,
   Than bread that honest toil may win,
Than blessings of the laden board,
   The food He gives within.

The lion and the raven die,
   They only ask life's common bread,
Our souls shall live eternally,
   And they too must be fed.

Then not alone for earthly food,
 Teach us with lisping tongue to pray ;—
The heavenly meat that makes us good,
 LORD, give us day by day.

37.

AND FORGIVE US OUR TRESPASSES, AS WE FORGIVE THEM THAT
TRESPASS AGAINST US.

WHEN thou art kneeling down at night,
 Beside thy mother's knee to pray,
And thinking over all thy sins,
 Done through the busy day;

Then call to mind thy brother's wrong,
 To strife by angry passions driven,
And in thy heart forgive him all,
 As thou would'st be forgiven.

Go, throw thy little arms around
 His neck, and kiss him tenderly,
Nor turn away with pouting lip,
 And sullen tearful eye.

Thou hast sinned more against thy GOD,
 Than ever brother sinned to thee ;
If He should turn away His face,
 How wretched would'st thou be.

Dost thou remember when thy LORD
  Hung on His cruel Cross so long,
How in His agony He pray'd
  For those that did Him wrong?

They nailed His hands, they pierced His feet,
  Their angry hearts no pity knew,
" FATHER, forgive them," was His cry,
  " They know not what they do."

Go, seek thy little brother's side,
  And press to his thy rosy cheek,
And whisper the forgiveness free
  He is too proud to seek.

Then as the brightest ray from heaven
  Doth on the glittering dewdrop fall,
Thy penitence shall be received,
  And GOD forgive thee all.

38.

AND LEAD US NOT INTO TEMPTATION.

THERE is a land where flowers are fair,
  And pleasant paths run through the woods,
But evil beasts are lurking there,
  And there the pois'nous adder broods.

If we were in that land afar,
  And for the sake of those sweet flowers,
Should wander where such dangers are,
  A cruel doom would sure be ours.

More foolish he, who to the way
  Of strong temptation turns his feet,
Who listens what the wicked say,
  Who looks on the forbidden sweet.

O! when we asked at morning hour
  That GOD would make us good to-day,
And keep us from temptation's power,
  Did heart and lip together pray?

Not, if we seek the dangerous spot,
  Where we are tempted most to sin,
If for a moment be forgot
  Our tempter, and the strife within.

He spreads his snares in every place,
  His voice is sweet, his arm is strong;—
LORD, keep us by Thy stronger Grace,
  Nor let our wavering feet go wrong.

39.

BUT DELIVER US FROM EVIL.

CHILD, ere thou wander forth to play,
  Thy LORD's Own words be duly said,
  That thou from sin and danger dread
Delivered be to-day.

The spirit dark that works within,
  Will whisper evil to thy heart,
  Will turn thee from the better part,
And tempt thy soul to sin.

Thou canst not tell what danger near,
  What sorrow never dreamed before,
  This one short day may have in store,
What sudden pain or fear.

As I have seen a boat go down
  In quiet waters suddenly,
  When not a wave was on the sea,
Nor in the sky a frown.

But happy still in all distress,
  The child that to his father flies,
  The heart that on its GOD relies
For strength and holiness.

GOD's glorious Angels watch him round,
  GOD's SPIRIT on his soul is shed;
  In vain the tempter's snares are spread,
He walks on guarded ground.

Why should he dread misfortune's blast,
  Why should he tremble at the foe,
  Or fear for pain, or shame, or woe?
His heart is anchored fast.

Like lily flower that to and fro
  Is tossed upon the waters wide,
  What cares it for the changeful tide?
Its root is firm below.

40.

THEREFORE I SAY, AMEN, SO BE IT.

So be it, LORD; the prayers are prayed,
  But still we pause on bended knee,
And lingering, though the words are said,
  Look fondly up to Thee.

So be it, LORD; let nothing bad
  Scatter our incense on the air,
No wandering thoughts that we have had
  Arise to cloud our prayer.

So be it, FATHER; yet awhile
   We hang upon Thy patient ear,
And in the brightness of Thy smile
   A moment tarry here.

Like one who on a cloudy day
   Has caught a glimpse of the blue sky,
And though the gleam have passed away,
   Still looks with longing eye:

Or like a strain of music sweet,
   That dies away in mountain ground,
Till one by one the hills repeat
   The solitary sound;

So down the full Church falls alone
   The Pastor's voice; it sinks, and then,
Sweet echo to that solemn tone,
   We breathe our soft "Amen."

J. MASTERS AND CO., PRINTERS, ALDERSGATE STREET, LONDON

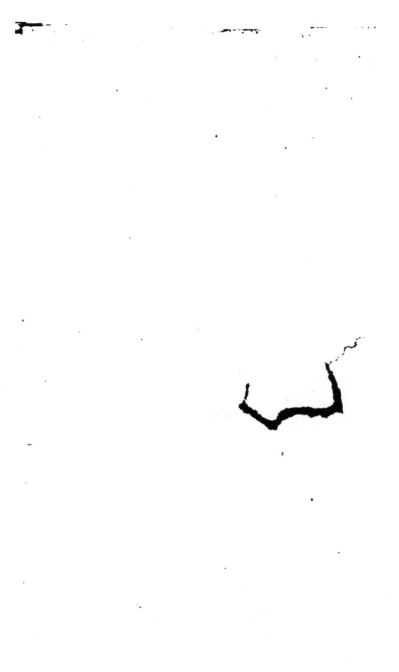

'1... The s.

down

CPSIA information can be obtained
at www.ICGtesting.com
Printed in the USA
LVHW082330070421
683556LV00016BA/16